The Dapples Of Darkness

The Dapples Of Darkness

Bhagaban Jayasingh

BLACK EAGLE BOOKS

7464 Wisdom Lane
Dublin, OH 43016
E-mail: info@blackeaglebooks.org
Website: www.blackeaglebooks.org

First published by
BLACK EAGLE BOOKS, 2019

The Dapples Of Darkness by Bhagaban Jayasingh

Copyright © **Bhagaban Jayasingh**

All rights reserved. No part of this publication may be reproduced, stored in a retrieval system, or transmitted, in any form or by any means, electronic, mechanical, photocopying, recording or otherwise without the prior permission of the publisher.

Cover and Interior Design: Ezy's Publication

Library of Congress Control Number: 2019938330
ISBN- 978-1-64560-004-6 (Paperback)

Printed in United States of America

For
Guddu, Dhanee and **Shyloo**
with love

CONTENTS

Subhadra and the Sea Beach	9
Among the Neanderthals	11
Address of a Girl's Floating Corpse to Her Rapist	12
Grandmother	14
Dak Bungalow	16
The Wound Inside My Heart	18
The Day My Father Died	20
The Whore	22
All Alone, in the Battlefield	24
Kakabaya	26
A Tale of Two Friends	28
To the Assassins of Innocence	30
Yet Another Hanuman	32
Playing with the Snake	34
Kalidas in the Encircling Net of Maya-1	36

Kalidas in the Encircling Net of Naya- 2	38
Life	40
Jayadratha's Delight	41
The Night Riding the Dog	43
Three Winter Gazals	46
The Sea From a Fisherman's Village	48
Just a Few Minutes Before Hanging	51
Manorama in a Rainy Night	53
Poet's Destiny	55
A Summer Shower in Cuttack	57
The Golden Axe	59
Now It's Time to Return Home	61
Purushartha	63
Revenge	65
Destination	67
Moin Khan, the Devil	69
Shadow Sex	71
Tiger in the City	73
The Tree's Address to the Woodcutter	75
The Cackle of Winter	77
The Day I Hang Up My Boots	79
Death at Midnight	81
The Morning Went Back	83
A Yogi at the Infamous Hut	85
The Muscleman	87

The Snake in My Garden	89
Confessions of a Crazy Man	91
Revengeful	93
History	95
Shehnai	97
The Bird of Eternity	99
After His Departure	101
Say Goodbye to the Poet	103
On an Officer's Superannuation	105
A Sea of Sorrows	107

Subhadra And The Sea Beach

The other day
I beckoned Subhadra to the sea beach
Leaning against a tall casuarina tree
that stood waist-deep in sand
I told Subhadra to steal a view of the sea
before everything turned topsy-turvy.

Subhadra was in a fix:
She could not know what to say
A handful of crabs encircled her
        waffle-thin waist
before a whiff of wind
could baffle her to the hilt.

Then Subhadra took my hand
with hers
and pressed her thigh against mine
A flock of birds flew away in fright
in anticipation of
something fearful happening.

The wind blew throughout the night
All the crabs and shells began to dissolve into the sand
The spotted deer bounced away
from the scene.

As I woke up from sleep
I found Subhadra was no more on the beach
The sea was not there among the shells
              and sand
There was no lustre in the emotions
The sea was floating in the sea water
like a chital fish in the pond.

Among The Neanderthals

It's not a place where one should live
among the neanderthals
of your untamed ego
staring into your bare bones
over the rocks,

where, even a bird, unsure
of its nest, flies away
flapping its wings against
the blue tantrums of
a landscape,

where knee-deep in the sun
your shadows mock
the emptiness of your ash
like a juggler bleeding history.

Yet, strong as ever
in my weakness for the flesh
I've shut down the doors to the wind;
I've no regrets
for bitterness of the blood

I'm happy where I'm.

Address Of A Girl's Floating Corpse To Her Rapist

Take me wherever you like
from near this river bank,
Put me in any posture you like
for your appetite
Or else fling me back to the river again.

Bodiless, I have no greed
for the body any more.
No more does my anger
drive the wind to avenge
your ruthlessness
Let the wind blow the way it likes.

Let your desire for my body, now
now a pile of petrified flesh, continue
to make you crazy: you can now
squeeze my breasts, touch my nipples
to whet your feline hunger.

You've thrown me into the river
means you have devastated me
put out all your lewd and lascivious thoughts
on my naked hips, to test
the crumpled patience of my cunt.

I don't mind if non-penitent,
you can move the world. I needn't have
to clench my teeth again against
your ponderous weight as

I' ve already crossed many mileposts
of your sick love, you can now
safely push your strength
into mine in a style of your own.

Grandmother

Grandpa died last night.
Soon after his departure
Grandma crushed her glass bangles
on a piece of stone
Then, she dropped back into a deep silence.

The vermilion mark on the parting
of her hair was gone,
The alta on her feet became wet with tears as blood,
The broken bangles showed
the drab and desolate picture of home.

I explained to grandma: How, once
ripe, the cucumber falls off its twig
on its own,
How the migratory birds fly back home
from Chilila at the end of winter.

It's not true that grandma does not know all about this.
Yet, she had never felt the agony of separation herself anytime before,
She had never measured out the depth of wounds beneath

her heart,
She felt like burning on the pyre here
when grandpa's body went aflame over there.

Grandpa is no more.
Grandma's blood has turned into water,
Her heart lies scattered in splinters
like the intricate entrails of a rotten calf on the road,
Her hands and feet get stuck up
in the deadly hole of a snake.

Grandma understands everything,
yet nothing;
She continues to ask: Why
Grandpa was here yesterday,
and why he does not exist today!!!

Dak Bungalow

The night would continue as before
First, you would hear its footsteps
like the anklets of a dancer
and then like a whiff of hot wind,
sense its invisible presence.

The ancestral windows of
the murky bungalow would begin to creak
for they would not stay unbroken
in their primeval positions;
The sound would be heard
of the roofs and walls crashing
in the darkness.

Scared, I would get up from bed
thinking of something weird happening
my wife shall get up from sleep,
and being sure that there was no one around
would slip into the bed again,
The environs would look frightening.

Who is calling? Why is calling?
When I would be still pondering
the door shall be flung open
with a deafening thud
The pigeons shall fly away from
under the bridge
The light shall go off the city.

Then the telephone would start ringing
and when I would place it on my ear,
someone someone would ask from
the other side, "Can't you place me?"
Then burst into peals of laughter
when my flesh would crawl in fright.

But, a little before dawn, I would
discover my wife was not on my bed
and a shadow continued stretching
beyond the pitch dark road
behind the broken walls.

The Wound Inside My Heart

Have you ever seen the wound
inside my heart?
Festering it has turned me into a carrion
that still continues to bleed
on every avenue of pain.

Look how the wound
which you have never seen
still remains alive and invisible
untouched of all my holdbacks,
without you knowing it.

The heart's mirror that reflected the moon
in all seasons of despair
has now broken into
thousand pieces, and each piece
crying out in pain
and spilling away blood like
a fountain

The river of tears blue with hurt
has swept away
the half-lit glass house in which I lived

that had once burnished my love
for decades
with the dappled lights of
chrysanthemums.

I am sure you shall come some day
and touch my wound
even for once
move your fingers through its pain,
and feel the heat of my burning flesh.

maybe a path in the forest
will open up among the groves of
mohul trees in blossoms
maybe when
life would call life
like a lark calling the morning
to touch the heel of the white sun.

The Day My Father Died

1.

Staring straight into your
still, blank and unblinking eyes
I called you out
but you could hardly hear me.
I ran my hand over your stubble
and nudged your chin
that carried the stains of the betel juice
dribbling out of your mouth

But you did not hear me.

The neighbours who gathered round you,
friends and relatives who came to see you,
shook your frail little arms
called you by various names

But you stared vacantly as never before.

Some people said
you shall not hear any more,
after some moments

your eyelids will shut
your breath will stop
your limbs will stop their movement
the wind will cease to blow.

Never shall you hear again.

2.

Several times did I stare at you
before I could place your lifeless body
on a few logs of wood
and light the pyre.

In the deep and dense silence of the cemetery
I tried to hear your call
through some invisible symbols
and holding my arms with yours
say, "Why worry my son, I'm here."

On my way back home after
I consigned your body to the rising flame
I felt you are walking right in front of me
with a stick clutched in your hand
and guiding me as before,

and at every crossroad telling me
how far has this road gone from here
how far has that road gone from there
And what is the distance of
All roads from here.

The Whore

Leaning against the cement-plastered wall
    as she stands
her hair gets decked up by the moon,
    the stars lay scattered all
over her half-naked body.

Her body exudes the magic of lust,
    her eyes carry
the desires of fulfilment,
    her love reflects
the complete surrender of
    volatile faith.

She gleans the mustard seeds
    of her fate from life's mosaic floor,
when her breasts excite the sterile sky
    streaming stars.

In the dimly lighted narrow lanes of her city,
    the clouds of hunger spread
like the deep sighs of a wounded sheep
    and the visitors burn
In the flames of envy and despair.

The darkness of night turns mad
    as it thickens on her aromatic hair,
the moon disappears for a while,
    when the flesh feeds the flesh
in the restless tranquillity
    of the dark night.

The non-fulfilment of her love
    cannot light the staggering shadows of
her womb
    as the clouds get lost in the arms of clouds
the roots do not turn into leaves
    and flowers into fruits
in unwelcome seasons.

Everyday the damsel stands
    leaning against the cement-plastered wall,
the spear of unrealised love
    tries to push through every fleshly cramp
in its search for fruition.

Accidents of darkness
happen always in her forbidden lane.

All Alone In The Battlefield

I stand on this battlefield
Alone--
after my valiant general has deserted
the army;
Kill me if you would
I've hardened my heart like
a stone.

The sun has set:
Blood from the wound has
coagulated on the general's
crackling chariot,
The sky looks hot as despair.

I understand:
I have to fight the battle alone
after so much of death and destruction,
and burn my dead companions
in the dead of night
Alone.

Then what
sorrow?

what
despair?
I have to fight through thick and thin
Alone
in spring and the storm.

I have not yet,
abandoned the arms,
Armoured to the hilt
and deeply entrenched I stand
with my soul bare
Kill me if you can
Kill.

Kakabaya*

I do not know where he lives.
But once the mother calls out his name
He scurries forward
Leaving his home among the bushes
or among the small copses
 of trees behind
          the dak bungalow.

He can mark some drops of tears
like pearls
freezing on the child's eyelids;
A clump of darkness
like some uneaten grains of rice
still clinging to her chin.

Hands black as tar,
Face, soaked in the river of blood,
Teeth like the white bones of a whale
always terrify her:
Yet, she bears them all
as the palasha of her ego
melts away in the dark.

Even though she wakes up
in the middle of the night
She cannot get herself free from the terror
of his oppression
The fear like a pack of dogs
barks at her all through the night.

Kakabaya is always insensitive.
He can never feel the child's plight.
But faithful to the mother
he only eagerly waits for her call
hiding among the bushes or the trees
      behind the dak bungalow.

Kakabaya enjoys to scare away children
at every call of mothers
who is always happy to make them dumb.
Who can understand the pains of the child
And the cruel malignity of the devil?
....

*Kakabaya is an imaginary image of a devil whom in every household a mother in Odisha calls by name to silence a very small child, particularly when it refuses to eat and sleep, etc.

A Tale Of Two Friends

I never did know my Friend
That this forest was so deep
Its green leaves were so cruel and fiendish
The forest path a repertoire of conflicts
And violence!

I never knew my trust of you
Could take the shape of a jungle
Our friendship become dry as hard stone
Your visible love transform into a warehouse
Of pretensions!

How come you called me to show
The loving pictures of the forest
The maddening images of the brooks
The flowers like malati, tamal, kurei and bakul!

Did I ever know my Friend that the bear
would arrive from nowhere,
And leaving me alone
you would climb up the tree,
I would lie on the forest floor
Like a corpse, waiting for my unknown fate!

Did I ever think that the bear would come
From nowhere and its wild breath
would ring like death in my baffled blood
It's cold cruel song would spread through
every lane and bylane of my arteries and veins
In every cell of my heart.

I never knew after the bear's exit
You would climb down from the tree
And with extreme caution or love ask,
"What did the bear whisper into your ears
My friend?"

What answer should I give my dear Friend,
Did I ever know how to define love and prove it?
But as I understand it's like finding
A sea right in front, a hunter at the back
On one side there's fire and on the other a net
"Is not it that friendship is like
A hunter's trap where a deer is caught unawares?"

Are you not the one my friend?

To The Assassins Of Innocence

Nobody knows how he walks
through the dark bones of despair
    heavy with the sounds of
    his empty soul sad as ever:
you never know how his road
    breaks at every turn of your lust.

He hangs between the fire and the hunter
like the lengthening shadows
    between the rocks and rumblers
    between the sun and the sword
when the river crawls its way
    to his ever receding destination.

Do you know how he splits
and shreds his destiny with stones
    which he pelts at his own images
    not mindful of the fiery rattles of guns
when you snore in your bed in
    the comforts of their impending death.

He is not aware how he eats the wild
oats of your greed night on night
    leaving behind the riches of
        home comforts tottering in cold
to build a skyscraper of dreams
    standing tall in the dredging rain.

I don't know when he will realise
your sinister design of shooting birds
    with arrows deadly as your desire,
        refuse to spill blood in the unforgiving
forest of repentance and wait for the god
    to bless the earth with love.

Yet Another Hanuman*

You thought
like the sparklers' light
in the dense, dark night
you would illuminate the stage.

You'll drown yourself
in the wild applause of the audience,
engrave immortality
on your parents' names.

You thought
like the leaves growing darkly
on the twigs in the moonlight,
you'll make the flowing stream
glow with your blood
and place the evening
on the sun's trajectory of fame.

Therefore you decked yourself
as Hanuman,
adorned your tail with deft hands,
set it aflame before
you jumped off the stage.

How come the fire spread across
to your liver and heart,
burning wildly your bones and blood
that deafened your scream
at dead of the night!

After you are gone
everything is still and quiet now,
I am on the audience gallery, alone,
like a desolate star in
the anguished sky,
I shall continue to wait till
you returned.

....

*The poem was written on the sad demise of a Calcutta schoolboy who burned himself to death while enacting the role of Hanuman in a school function.

Playing With The Snake

> I love to walk in rain because no
> one can see my tears.
> -- Charlie Chaplin,
> Famous British comic actor

While playing with the snake
    On the terrace
Bhabanath never knew that
    The snake would bite him so hard!

Yet, before its poison
Travelled fast into his heart
He stood on the parapet
To revel in the coming rain.

Darkening the surrounding
Arrived the rain
Bhabanath thought he would wear
Anklets of rain to dance on the terrace.

Just in moments, spell of the rain
Began to caress my body

Its magic spread across the city
Bhabanath had completely forgotten
That the snake had stung him!

He danced and danced for an hour
Till the rain beat a retreat to its nest,
The sunlight began to wrap the city
Uniting all its roads together,
But before Bhabanath could realise
The snake had slithered away from the spot.

Now-a-days, Bhabanath has understood
How, in order to live one has to play with
The snake, burn in its poison,
And hide death behind the curtain
Of rain water.

Kalidas In The Encircling Net Of Maya- 1

Is not this world a narrow bridge?
Tread softly on this bridge
Kalidas!
Don't please build a house on it.

Or else, the bridge might crumble
someday
The house might collapse into the river below
Time will carry away all your dreams and hopes
and destroy your love.

Sail your boat slowly, Kalidas!
Don't please differentiate
between the river and a mountain
A patch of rice field from a pile of pebbles
under a faint moonlight.

What is hereafter?
Which wealth?
Which skyscraper?
Which Time?
What love for fulfilment?

Can you save yourself from
the biting nails of Kalapurusha, the destroyer,
Who knows how one day
it will lead you to a tunnel
And morph you into the darkness of ash!

Remember, therefore, Kalidas
The world is a bridge
Tread softly over it
Don't please build a house on it.

Kalidas In The Encircling Net Of Maya- 2

Sometime, before the night
climbed down the ladder of dawn,
someone knocked on my door and called
in a harsh and sweet voice:

"Wake up Kalidas, wake..."
when my daughter clasped my hand
in utter, innocent terror.

Then, the stranger
hummed a different tune, his voice
sounded like a lizard's,
his wild breath frightening away
the wakeful birds in their nests.

I thought I could open the door
and in the pre-dawn candle light
stare intently into his face
touch the silence of his flesh
that hardly feels
the pains of our mortal frame!

Can he understand
the burden of man?
sufferings of the broken heart?
Does he know
why the seedlings wilt
without the sunlight of love?

What have I wished from life?
Have I ever tried to embellish it
with rangani flowers of fulfilment
the priceless jewellery of joy
a pail of water from the lake of happiness?

I know this body is not me
This mind is not me
This breath is not me
The blood that safely traverses
my veins and arteries is not me.

Still, O stranger!
Please stop to knock on my door.
Don't you know I am Kalidas
I am still not ready to tear asunder the veil.

Life

I don't have any such plan to live
Let my life move the way it feels fit.

I have nothing to gain from life
Nothing to lose from life either
It's all the same whether I lose or gain.

No matter who is with me or not
I have drawn the curtain on everything
I have nothing ecstatic to feel about in love
Nor have I anything disheartening to feel in
                hate
I have climbed up the hills alone.

I don't know what's in store for me in life
Still I have to set the wax-house on fire
Forget to prop a ladder to heaven
And stir a life among the seven-layered silts.

Let no one remember me after I'm gone
Let no one place a flower bouquet
    on my grave
I was never alive while dying
I'm already dead while living.

Jayadratha's Delight

The war had come to an end
before I stepped into the room
Jayadratha, the valiant hero,
had sent the butterfly to the ground
The sky looked wild from the window.

All over the floor lie scattered
butterfly's bones, some blood,
broken bangles and excitement
The rain has gone back
After touching the window
The sky feels wet.

The room is dumb:
It cannot speak out what
has happened inside it
The traveller has gone away
In a fast-moving train.

Everything is quiet now.
in the room's pale light
the fan has stopped moving
the bones of restlessness
have filled the entire room.

The citizens of the city are asking:
What has happened inside the room?
What has really happened?
"No, no, nothing has happened," someone
      said,
Only Jayadratha, delighted by
the untimely sunset, has gone back
in the night under the pouring rain."

The Night Riding The Dog

This poem was written on an actual experience in a dark, rainy night. I was waiting for a bus at Balasore to go to Bhadrak, a distance of about 60 kilometers. By mistake, I boarded a bus that was plying on a different route.The conductor asked me to get down from the bus when the mistake was discovered, but not before the bus had already covered about 10 to 15 kilometres. The road back to the city looked frightfully lonely and desolate in the surrounding gloom of the dark night. Scared to the bone, as I began to walk along the road, without the sight of any man or habitation, I could feel someone following me from behind. As I turned back, to my utter disbelief but to a great relief, I could see an unusually huge dog following me at a little distance. It maintained a regular distance, and stopped if I stopped to look back at it. Although the distance the dog accompanied me till it disappeared near a wayside pond on the well-lighted outskirts of the city.

It was well past midnight.
The conductor made me
step out of the bus. He planted some
frail legs of dead crabs on my palm,

a wreath of bones and skulls
of snails around my neck.

After I got down
the bus sped away
on its destination. The rain-hurt night
appeared like a bunch of wet
skeletons hanging on the tall deoders
in the dark.

The water boiled over in my brain
as my feet began to freeze
in my heart. Hairs stood on end.

Like fireflies the distant city
glimmered in the surrounding gloom
of the night. The roadside trees
bent forward frighteningly
at me like apparitions.

"How would I cross the distance
How?" as I thought to myself
the earth slipped off my
feet. The night rose and fell
in my nerves.

Before I could stop thinking
the environs burst into
a wild laughter. Before
I could do something
a shadow stood before me
straight and simmering

in the rain-baffled night.

At the turn of the scene
I felt I was not inside me
my outside was not inside me
and a huge dog was carrying
me forward and I rode
safe on its back.

And when I regained consciousness
I had already reached my destination
and the dog had melted
into thin air.

Three Winter Gazals

One

Winter, as I caress you
I feel you are
The thrill of my rhymeless nights
You are an an exile of anxious blood.
You are the crazy moonlight
Over the long recognised hill
Of memories.

Two

Winter is a night of separation.
With its cold kisses
Tremble the bones
Its hairy wishes
Embellish many a mind
Its mellifluous voice
Makes the wicks of blood
Light my lonely chamber of despair.

Three

After winter exits
The city's neon lights will be extinguished
The pride of fog will die down
On every blade of grass
The commotions will end on roads
Who knows if suddenly winter
Will return to announce
"I've not gone
I'm still there in your blood."

The Sea From A Fisherman's Village

1.

The sea looks exactly like
a fisherman boy
naked and vibrant
whose back the sunrays
bast as a cruise missiles
everyday,
burn his body black.

At a small distance from
the fisherman's village
the wind wafts in their sighs of sorrow
as the sinister stench
spreads across the sea
the stench of the burning flesh.

The smoke and dust emanating
from the dog fights
turn into rotten sea fish;
the broken bones of sharks
floating among the beating waves
remind the sea of its inner violence.

Yet, the fisherman lives
in a style of his own
though the sea recedes
like a young calf
from its sick mother
and distance carries him
on his cart of despair.

2.

The fishes have no season.

They come in the sun and the rain
In the storm and the cyclone
they offer themselves
to be caught in the fisherman's net
they wallow in their uncompromising surrender.

The fishermen have no season.

Everyday
they indulge in shooting the fish
with their arrows which never miss the target
make them senseless
mercilessly kill them all.

Yet, fish are the friends of fishermen.

Fishermen's future
stands secure on their bones
their faces look like the photographs
of their eyes
quiet and uninterested.

O Fishermen!

Look at the sea in front of you
its womb is full of fishes of various colours
why wait then
mount your arrow on the bow
raise your axe
let the void tremble

O you hunter!
Begin your bloodshed.

Just A Few Moments Before The Hanging

After sometime
A cruel sound will push me far
Far from the venom of commotion of this world
Very far.

I shall drift away
Like the mad, turbulent stream
Of a river in spate
Pushing behind me
Many a confusion of
Many familiar villages and cities.

After a while
The candlelight will be put out
In the yet-to-blow wind
Darkness will come pushing in
Like a sharp, bloody knife.

A sudden and certain terror
Will blend in the air
The tears of empathy and anxiety
Will dissolve on the face.

A fearful wind
Will whip against the trees
The blood will clot in the heart
After a deadly snake bite.

The trust of of my friends and
Relatives will melt away
No longer shall the lotus bloom
In the rainwater of their assurances.

The milk from my wife's nipples
Will dry up on its own
The uncertain future of my children
Will hang on the sharp edge of a sword.

Just a few moments after this
A dark storm will push me
Far, very far
And what can make the earth, the womb of violence, tremble for some unknown peace!!!

Manorama In A Rainy Night

Yesterday, in the middle of the night
    Manorama called me me up,
the frogs began to croak in unison
    soon after the phone rang.

Manorama said she was alone
    it was raining hard and her husband
had not returned from a 5-day sojourn
    in a foreign land,
and there was no chance of his return
    in 5 days from now.

Manorama happily took me inside
    as soon as I knocked at her door,
locked her arms with mine
    her lips with mine;
I could hear thunder in a distance.

Soon after the thunder struck
    everything turned dark
under the spell of darkness Manorama
    burned like a ball of fire
Atmosphere sounded mysterious
    and beyond control.

Soon after I shot an arrow
    that flew up into the air
The red hot eyes of Manorama swelled
    to take the shape of a globe;
In moments
    Manorama lost her senses.

By the time Manorama opened her eyes
    the sun had already sunk into the horizon,
love had lost all her excitement.
    only the sound of an owl screeching
was flying in the air
    from the tall branch of a shami tree.

Poet's Destiny

Why should a poet write poetry
when he will have to fade into oblivion
like a leaf after the tree sheds it in winter?

Remaining awake for the whole night
writhing in excruciating pain
why should he write poetry
when darkness might engulf the earth
digging a grave in the heart.

Why should he connect
the blossoms with their stems
place the roots on the soil
eyes with the eyes;
A sudden bolt from the void
might devastate the forest of his luck.

Why should he bleed to death
scooping out an image
from among thousands of words;
the strings of his poetry might snap
without the real meaning of his verse.

There is no use for the poet
to grope in the seed's darkness;
Being blighted with the seed's curse
the tree might burn itself to death
before its tendrils died in the cold blisters.

Why should he try to stop a river
midstream which he thinks his pen can do;
The wilderness of breath might turn to
a cyclone of silence
the snow might melt into the darkness of death.

Thousands of years might pass
but unsatiated in his quests
the poet will still remain
eternally hungry and helpless
Then why should he light
the earthen wicks of his hopes?

A Summer Shower In Cuttack

It's a summer afternoon in Cuttack
the colourless westerly wind
beats against the wayside trees
whose weak branches try to kiss
the dry land with the hope of
a shower of heavy rain.

The gossamer threads of the clouds
as they stretch forward to cover
the city, the birds shriek flitting
from branch to branch
I do not know why Mandakini feels
lonely in her solitary home now.

The dry leaves swing in
the wind as the storm of dust rises
in the city of mosques and the temples
spreading the stench of the drains
inflicting a wound on the breasts of
a girl returning from school.

The firecrackers of thunder
as they roar in the city creates tremors

down its spine like Manorama's love
which had seared her heart
when rain's knife had pieced
the entire city in the dark.

The rain begins to pour in showers
darkening the city streets making the ants
helpless and wetting the sloughs
of snakes and lengthening
my fear for life that once hit me hard
                        in the past.

The Golden Axe

1.

As the axe fell down into
the river water
while felling the tree,
the water nymph asked,
"Is this your axe?"

The water nymph held
in her palm a bunch of tarat flowers
thee magical ash of the future.

The woodcutter shook his head
and said, "No"
in a clear and intelligible voice.

Sinking into a deep despond
Greed began to retire from the scene
as he could not bring
under his spell a chunk of light
like the woodcutter.

2.

The next day,
Looking at the golden axe
on the water nymph's hand
that sparkled like the bright disc of the sun
The woodcutter's brother said,
"Yes, the axe is mine."

Even before his words came to an end
The sky became dark
Thunder roared frighteningly
over the riverbank.

At a distance, unrestrained,
Greed began to giggle:
How could the body's ash
ignore the strange rules of the world?

Now It's Time To Return Home

Now it is time to return home.

Meanwhile I have travelled many miles
Crossing through
Many forests of my desires.
I have made numerous compromises
With the wicked winds of darkness
In apprehension about
My uncertain future.

Who knows what is going to happen next
The thief might arrive at any moment
Shoot his arrows of abuses at me
Mirror might break into thousand pieces.

These days I'm not able to
See my face in the mirror
Not even your face.
Its glass has already picked up some dust and moss
The boat has toppled over midstream.

I have come to the house means
I've to go to the house
Cool the burning fire within my heart
In every fall of a meteor
Make everybody understand
Who I am
And who are you?

Look how I'm in a house
That looks like a boat
Without ores
I don't know where this rudderless boat
Take me to
I don't know when I can reach my house
In a moonlight-spangled night!

Purushartha

I do not know who he is.
Yet, my manliness lies in following
His footsteps
I know it for sure
You believe or not.

I am aware
That I have to run after him
Through all ages
In this life and after.
Robeless in his desires
Become hapless
Like false promises.

I do not know what was there before me
What is there in store hereafter
But I have to run means
I have to cross many mileposts
And reap my karmic fruits.

I have not known as yet
Who I am
I do not know

Who you are
Who he is
Why am I running
After the unattainable?

You may say
I am helpless
You can ask me for its reasons
You might point your finger
At the bird
That has fallen off the sky
While flying.

But please wait
Before the bird gains back its strength
To fly into the sky
Before the sky conspires to
Impair its will to move

I will prove my manliness to one and all
You believe or not.

Revenge

After the end of the ghat road
Scared
I looked around,
There was none except for a couple of birds.

The boss with his cold, cruel gaze,
Stared into my eyes
From a king-size photo frame
Exactly the way he looks at me,
Or roars over my every small mistake.

Once again, I threw my eyes
On the image of the boss
A thin trail of dread travelled across my heart
Yet I consoled myself: Aye, it's not the boss
A photograph only.

I hung the photograph on a tree trunk.
Lest it should fall down,
Strengthened it with strong and sharp nails;
Put a garland of shoes round his neck
And screamed: Shala, where
Should you go now?

Then I went on hitting it
With my shoes, one after the other,
Leading the picture finally to fall off the trunk,
And the scraps of blood-soaked papers
Flying around the forest
And was finished soon.

That night, with extreme caution, I whispered
Into the my wife's ear, "Do you know darling!
Someone has murdered the boss
And flung his body down in the forest."

Destination

I do not know who'll accompany me
to the emptiness
to those dark caves of terror,
except perhaps, in crumpled form
my self, none will glide
on the corridors of time
accompanying a frail frame
to its destination.

This destination was never
my end, since I hardly believe
in deliverance. How can
an experience without a mouth
spit venom against
the landmines of cruelties
serve me and my interest
to linger on here even
in the unserving chill!

I do not know whether
I could meet history there
sitting like a plump whore
of confusions, always, deluding

the innocents like me
tempting them to believe in
what they should not.

A worshipper of dark reasons
I always think of emptiness
as yet another form of my self
the ash-laden memories
of casuarinas on the sea.

You might not accompany me
but I'll have to go there,
share the discomforts of all
who are always there;
and suffocated, again, like them,
follow their shadows in the dark
to a place where someone

his face radiant with cruelties, like
a headmaster's, will thrash me
with his cane as he always does
to the errant boys.

Moin Khan, The Devil

The road, hereafter, winds
a little further and after a furlong or so
it terminates in a forest

where, encircled by a mighty army
of stupid stooges, a sinister brood
of warmongers, lives the demon,
30+, black and 5 ft 9 inches tall.

I have never seen the demon
except in wee hours of
the shattered dreams when darkness
like a huge spaniel barks at
the crude deceit of the moon.

A hungry jaw of death, he tears
into the flesh of my unlearned
                    conscience,
my idea of love and hate
that soars in the wind during the day
till the sun bids a goodbye to
a brewing hurricane.

Moin Khan, the devil,
snaps at every weakness
that guards him with deadly weapons
of stars atop all mou mountains
under snow.

I do not love him as much as he hates you
for your every act of empathy.

Yet I do not know why I feel
him in every ounce of my blood
touch him in every whiff of my breath
and this reality never deludes
me like the far-off mountains
among the nightingales.

Shadow Sex

It was difficult to know
who was that shadow that spent the night
with Manorama.

The bright moonlight that
shone so brightly outside her house
could hardly penetrate the darkness
inside.

Manorama looked hot and glamorous.
Her red lips and bare legs
spread out the fragrance of
some raw flesh;
her cheeks and chin offered unfamiliar thrills
of many uncanny nights.

It was not known
whether Manorama was inside the shadow,
or the shadow was inside Manorama
but the winds crashed around
with several shrieks
in every gesture of body.

At daybreak
it was found that the shadow
had melted away
at the first touch of sunlight,
the hunter had gone back to his forest home,
but Manorama was still lying in bed
exhausted to the bone.

Tiger In The City

Throughout the day
and although the night
They went on a massive search for the tiger
through all the lanes and bylanes
hills of clutters,
drains looking like creeks
and bushes creating the impression
of mangrove forests.
But the tiger was nowhere to be seen.

After being assured
that the tiger was not there in the city
The news editor of an unknown channel
focussed their camera
on a few anxious onlookers
and asked: "Have you seen the tiger?"
The townsmen laughed
like an intelligent boy before
a foolish teacher.

Like the newly-married bride
asking Dibyalochan in the honeymoon night
The people of the city

asked each other
"Have you seen the tiger?"

Some drew up the image
of the tiger on the floor in chalk
Some others stuffed sulphur and fire
into the eyes of a monster.

Suddenly
The rain accompanying blasts of thunder
came crowding into the city
The current went off the city
In a few moments
The tiger appeared on the scene
from the constable Karuna Barik's backyard
and roared: "You fools, are you
searching for the tiger?
Then look within
Yes very much within your self,"

The Tree's Address To The Woodcutter

The sound of your cutting
reaches here echoing through every leaf,
my heart begins to tremble
as the sound of a siren rings through
my every nerve and vein,
sweats flow from top to bottom
with the speed of lightning.

Everywhere echoes your animal voice
in every hollow of a hill,
in every corner of the sky,
in every river, canal, valley and fountain
a terrible dread passes through
my stunned roots
in my blood boils the fire of your violence
it makes the heart disfigured and grey.

Now listen you Woodcutter
my dreams have not come to an end
half of my life has not been spent

my body has not bloomed yet
life's thirst has not been quenched
I have still miles to go in rain and sunshine.

Why are you so cruel, O Woodcutter
forgetting the greatness of love and
                friendship,
can't you see how my trunk trembles?
how the naked sound of death is everywhere
in heaven earth, sky and hell?

Go back, Woodcutter today
give me back my rights to live in my dreams
try to understand life's meaning
through its relationship with death
and give me O you Woodcutter
some song of love of this loving night
some ripples of love of this life.

The Cackle Of Winter

When winter, like a middle-aged woman in rags,
was asleep on the desolate street,
my doorbell went off
and startled, I woke up from the bed.

The wall-clock then struck a quarter past two.
Being tormented by the deepening cold
my bones began to rattle,
flutters of the vulture's wings
were heard from the nearby banyan tree
at the village end.

The cold got on my nerves
and engulfed my entire body
from top to toe;
but before I could make out
who could call me at such an hour
the doorbell rang again.

My hands trembling
I went up to open the door,
there was none except the surrounding
that hissed like a female cobra
with its fangs ready to sting.

A quick stab of dread
bled me unawares,
Shivering I could hear winter's cackles;
blood froze in my tangled veins
just when dis-attired, the winter
stood like a middle-aged woman
freezing in front of my house
in the thickening fog.

The Day I Hang Up My Boots

No more have I to bend
my head in sheer subservience
before the king and call him
the maker of my destiny
emperor of my sick love and sins.

In the crowd of crazy cowards
I do not have to stand any more
with folded hands for a living
and pretend to honour
the direful devilry of his whims.

Now I am the king, the monarch,
the imperator of my impulses
the sovereign ruler of my world
till shivering I fall to the ground
by the axe of a fraudulent crank.

Hereafter I have to laugh
in the teeth of your passion
coax your blood in the night without moon
tame the wild beasts of your lust
through the half-forgetful lines
of our sacred texts.

I know: hereafter I have to
spin my own cocoon,
re-glue my broken foot
forgive my unrequited love
enjoy pampered lyrics on dead lips
that once sang my story of
love to the blood moon.

I am free now, yes, free as the wind
that soughs through the spring leaves
My world looks bright as
the wild hyacinths on the lake
I am happy that I am to hang up my boots
today in the afternoon
when I am not still not ready to die.

Death At Midnight

>Beginning today, treat everyone you
>meet as if they were going to be
>die by midnight. Extend to them all
>the care, kindness and
>understanding you can muster, and
>do it with no thought of any reward,
yout life will never be
>the same again.
>
>**Og Mandino**
>American author

As I looked at him
I felt he would go away this midnight
Some drops of tears rolled down my cheeks
A fierce fire engulfed my body.

It was midnight.
His coffin was ready.
I thought he might exit any moment from now.

The cruel Kalapurusha
had started calling aloud

From the end of the village
The devil was out in the open
to sting with his demonic fangs.

The unrestrained flow of
blood congealed in my heart
The snakes slithered back
into their holes in fright.
The night looked horrendous as never before.

I was sure he would go this midnight.

The clock struck 12.
A fierce wind that blew
in that moonless night
Tore down the flag atop the temple.
I got ready to carry the coffin myself.

On my way to the beach
Where I had to consign him to flame
I felt that the gentleman was not in the coffin
The coffin was not on my shoulder
A band of pirates were pulling
My dead hands

towards the burning pyre.

The Morning Went Back

The morning descended
right in front of the temple
and called,
    "Wake up you God!"

The priest whose eyes were
still saddled with last night's sleeplessness
called:
    "Wake up you God!"
The arrow of pain was stuck up in his body
that stretched across his soul.

Suddenly a loud scream of shock
startled the nearby anla tree
As it saw a poisonous snake
crawling inside the hollow of its trunk
with a chic clutched firmly in its mouth
It called:
    "Wake up you God!"

The lewd and lascivious merchant
of the city, who carried a flower pot for
offering that contained vermillion

of adultery, false devotion to God
madness of loot, blood of exploitation
called:
    "Wake up you God!"

At the temple's backyard
The frock-wearing body of
the school going girl was still hung
from the champak tree;
But city rulers closed their eyes
though the clues of murder and the murderer
flew in the wind
An onlooker called:
    "Wake up you God!"

But the God did not wake up
as though nothing has happened,
and nothing is going to happen in his world!
The morning went back
on the unclear avenues of the city
hatred began to travel
like an indifferent night of spring.

A Yogi At An Infamous Hut

He never knew it was not
just a polythene hut
but a sinister thatch of corrupt flesh
a certain tunnel to the hell

where, alone, lived the woman
more a sketch than flesh
that looked spent-up and sunken
in that moonless night of the jackals.

Unaware of the ways of the flesh,
he knocked on the makeshift door
perhaps to escape the chill-soaked touch
of the winter rain.

But the woman, just freed from
the nightly burdens, stared into
the eyes of the man she had never seen before
who looked unmoved and cold
in his saffron apparels.

"No more, I'm tired" -- she yelled
not knowing that the man who stood

motionless and still beyond
the boundary of the tumultuous world
was a yogi shivering in rain.

Not angry nor perplexed, as usual,
the yogi said nothing
but the cold night air that still hovered
over the polythene hut0
reminded him of the ways in which
flesh yields to the defeats of the flesh
                      and death.

The Muscleman

The power of your strong arms
can set the flower trees ablaze
the land can cross the sea,

The sea can crush the land.
Today your limitless riches
have morphed you into an MLA,

Tomorrow you can become a minister
the next day a prime minister.
You can silence your critics at gunpoint,

Completely devastate your foes.
You are now monarch of your whims
you have united all that what we call evil

You have committed rape after murder
or murder after rape
yet, your patriotism the bugle blares

Throughout the country
and the people cannot have an inkling
of your conspiracy.

Look how you can beckon a deluge
to envelope a city,
burn the temple with

The firepower of your intolerance.
Look, how hapless look the deities
in their temple

And are ready to run away from it!
You are the ringmaster of circus.
you have tamed a pride of lions,

Spread the worms of helplessness
throughout the state.
Who knows when Kalapurusha would call

During the daytime,
and the entire city would remain calm
for the last rites of gods?

The Snake In My Garden

Uninvited,
he slithers through my gate.
And his arrival scratches out
a new map for my garden;
emotions of dread course
through my blood like poison.

A commotion, like lightning,
that spreads across my home
takes everyone unawares
The wind of naked apprehension
Turns into a cyclone of horror.

Wielding half-crushed twigs
as lathis in hand my son
and his friend throng the garden;
The stranger appears as an assassin
to each of the anxious moments
when helpless and absurd looks
the face of my garden.

As they chase the stranger
on his every move

crawling under the grass
the monkey of terror gibbers at him,
the shadow of death stands
at every footfall.

After hours
the sun sinks into the unquiet horizon
The evening sky begins
to darken the surroundings
Dull death hurries back
disappointed to the core.

Every time he comes
he spreads awe in my home
with his unlooked-for appearance,
but before blood cools
he slithers quietly back into his hole.

After his each departure
I continue to wait for his next arrival.

Confessions Of A Crazy Man

Who Dared A Lonely Woman

It caught her unawares.
Unprepared to shallow
the heaven's goodness
she hissed like a snake.

Battered to the bone
he began to sink but still
desperate not to let it go
he dared look at her kainch-red eyes
spewing fire.

With a heart still trapped
in the simmering sand
he folded his hands;
even when the candles of his adventure
were flickering away
to the blow of a violent wind.

Unable to stand any more
he began to move:
his guilt-heavy footsteps

creaking on
the rust-laden doors of the hell,
of course not until
he could hear a sweet familiar voice
cajoling him to stop.

As he looked back
to his disbelief and horror,
he saw the woman
standing stark naked by the bed
like a fleshly whore
in the sun.

Revengeful

I could not know why the ship,
Before it could cross the bar,
stopped midway.
The eyes of the captain, who never
knew what fear was,
welled up with the tears of dread.
The dawn broke in the middle of the night.

Whom should I trust now?
The show has come to a grinding halt
before it took off,
Death could strike hard before
one could lock
his arms with the arms of a
Pretty damsel.

What should love do now
except to stand non-penitent
in front of the queer pretensions of heart?
And what should heart do now
except to forgive the infertility of love?

Let us paint a picture of illusion
with the brush of faith
and break the bridge for a river of pain.
in the depth of a night.
Engage in some intimate moments
of fornication.

The ship can reach any time now.
Tons and tons of dead fishes
are floating in the waves
A fearsome sound of neighing
has started coming from every side.

The face of the captain looks
red as kaincha now.
An opportune moment has reached
to avenge
Death has started calling death since long.

History

Sometimes history changes its course.

The cold tune of death
rings through the rivers and highways,
months and dates
The lost prince of another time
comes back to see the angelic throne
swinging before his eyes.

Sometimes history changes its course.

In the way changes politics, governance,
the fate of the roadside beggar;
the way Ananta, son of the widow,
drives away in his own car
won from a ten-lakh lottery; yesterday's
a frail, little boy flaunts a knife
and Inflicts a deep wound on
a poor clerk while returning from
a late-night show.

Sometimes history changes its course.

Bismay Bal, the only son of his father,
who was once an incarnation of innocence,
now lives on fish, flesh and fowl
and teaches his half-drunken students
the theories of love, commonplace love.

Sometimes history changes its course.

In the way our face changes after
two pegs of whisky when the moon
looks lifeless, absent, the tree an apparition,
and the nearby church
a hotel's a security guard, old with years.

As Nietzsche, the philosopher, believed,
it is for a hundred years since the God is dead
and since then no leaves have come
upon the tree nor the flowers have bloomed
no clouds have danced on the sky's floor
When forests are flooded with rain water.

Everything changes for sure:
the relationship between life and death
the conflict between luck and lucklessness
as though it were the single most trait
of the society, this world, of this life.

Is God history and
there is nothing you cannot do
to undo the course of history?

Shehnai

Many days have passed
since I abandoned the river bank
and you forsook its ghat
Yet, we are now at the same place
separate from each other
by a paper wall.

Over the years my hair has turned grey
Flesh has stopped singing the praise of
           bones
The little bird that had built nest on the tree
has shifted to the nearby woods.

Beating a drum
among the flecks of clouds
the moon has beaten a retreat
The horizon has lost its verve
in the subtle flow of emptiness.

Upstream flows the river now
under the stainless clouds in lifeless spires
I don't have words for every grief
that a tree feels when it falls in the forest
in silence of the dreary nights.

Do you know why the wound
has not healed for years
Even after the stars had slid onto
the courtyards of our hamlets
The blood has congealed in the veins.

Look, we are at the same place as before.
You on the river bed and I on the ghat
We can hear the the sounds of
shehnai blaring an ancient tune of
our togetherness in wilderness.

The Bird Of Eternity

We have to go someday
melt into the ether of eternity
A white swan will glide over the lake
to find its utmost edge.

Someone will have to shoot
the dead man's shadow
stamped out against the sky
when the earth will be wet with grief
of the wounded bird.

I have to call out in a loud voice,
Come, I can bear it no more:
the terror of the wolf on the mohul flowers,
the spectacle of a forlorn village
            in the roaring rain
the agony of the tired flesh after a wild sex.

You can hear me or not
You may come out or not
But I have to go in search of
a foetus for my next birth,
a fort beyond this fort,
Anyhow I have to reach there.

Someone will escort me there inside,
give me new dresses to wear
after a cool bath
put a garland around my neck
a sandalwood mark on my forehead
kohl in my eyes when

A sweet cool voice will be heard
in the space
A ball of virgin light will fly away from
Inside the fort.

After His Departure

After his departure
The clouds have come back to
break into rains.

The environ that looked deadly
has returned to relish
every drop of rain of intimacy
between you and I.

Because I love to get drenched in rain
I stand with folded hands
before life for the sins
I have never committed.

Is it my sin that
I can't bear the weight of sorrow
hurtling down the street?
I can't bear a woman weeping at night
when sorrow begins to stroll along
the river bank in pain?

It's good that he has gone
not to return any time soon
But whether he comes or not
I continue to stand here as before
like a sinless criminal
with folded hands before life.

Say Goodbye To The Poet

Henceforth, stop to write poetry
You have already written a lot
You have already spoken a lot
babbling your absurdities
in devastating prose.

You have never climbed up a mountain
Nor have you ever seen it once
Then, why do you scoff at the man
who enjoys a night of the moon
on the mountain top?

Have not you smoked enough
in the company of gays in
nightclubs among the drunkards?
Have not you indulged enough
in the noontime tryst with whores
at a sleazy motel?

You have never touched
the subtle nerves of pain,
nor stirred a dying beggar's soul
felt the horror of a hurricane

Then, why do you beat the drum
that you are a poet of great substance?

Now, please wake up, leave the road
for the youth to follow
allow them to put a fresh wreath
of flowers on your photograph

Goodbye Brother!
Your time is up.

On The Officer's Superannuation

Go if at all you want to go
But before your exit at least have
a glance on the infamy of your misdeeds
which like wildfire has not
extinguished as yet.

Before your departure see
the powerlessness
of banana leaves of your ego
drifting away in the wild currents of power
Their desperation like one of salt
It's cruel assault on wound.

Many a time have I seen you
from far and near
throwing away the distance
in the frolicsome antics of the nearness
or the poverty of nearness
In the distance's unpretentious pranks.

Have not you realised
how inexcusable has been

your execution of power
How uncompassionate
are your compassions!

Go wherever you like to go,
Go,
We will celebrate your absence
with all the delectables in a grand feast
The atmosphere will be romantic
with a variety of tasteful dishes.

But you will not be here
The joy of your being not here
will spread like virtues from birth to birth
in the destiny of all the unfortunate ones
like us.

The Sea Of Sorrows

The horizon between
the sea and the sky
encircles my sorrows
stretching over miles of land;
The wind blows away
the perfumes of a frozen intimacy.

Time whacks its way
into the void of my life
The lonely sighs of a treacherous love
sear my heart:
Tempered with hate
It wets my
sea of sorrows.

A frightful season
that has robbed the hillsides cuckoo
of its music
torments me with lewd thoughts
that I cannot resist
at the sight of the sea waves
beating against the shore.

Now I have layers of sorrows:
they confront me
with the daggers that can

split my heart into several pieces;
Death rises to meet
every face it hates.

Sorrow is a kind of death:
It is like a boy lying on the beach
with outstretched arms;
I do not know why
I have to die at the approach of
spring and be one with the boy
on the beach.

Darling!
Help me smile a little
at least for the sake of my child
in your womb
Look how life dribbles out
like drops of tears in the eyes
of the hillside cuckoo;

when a throbbing emptiness
of my drab existence
rumbles at me like a monkey
and the sea wind burrs on
the casuarina's spurred branches
to give a feeling
what life is!

Darling
Will you please smile a little
to save the sailor from drowning?

www.ingramcontent.com/pod-product-compliance
Lightning Source LLC
Chambersburg PA
CBHW052103070526
44584CB00017B/2315